Origins

Treasure Hunt

Chris Powling ✳ Jonatronix

OXFORD
UNIVERSITY PRESS

In this story...

Max

Cat

Ant

Tiger

Miss Jones

Lucy

2

Also in this story...

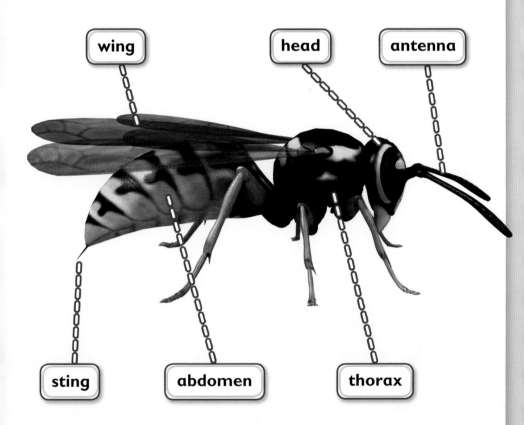

wing

head

antenna

sting

abdomen

thorax

Wasps have a sting in their tail. They use it to defend themselves. They can sting people too so watch out! A sting can be painful but is not normally dangerous.

Wasps like sweet things like fruit, jam and chocolate.

Chapter 1 - The clue

It was the day of the pirate fair at school.
Miss Jones had set up a treasure hunt.
A crowd of excited pirates jostled round her.

"Remember the pirate code," she said, as she handed out the first clue. "All pirates must share their booty."

To find the next clue
Here's what to do
Head to the east
Where children can feast

Tail on the Parrot

"Share it?" said Cat. "We've got to find the booty first!"

"That could take forever," grumbled Tiger. "This is just a clue to find another clue!"

Lucky Sand Pit Treasure Dip

"And you need to be really clever
to solve a puzzle set by Miss Jones,"
said a voice.

Max, Cat, Ant and Tiger groaned.
It was Lucy.

"So I will be the winner," said Lucy,
loudly. "I'm the cleverest pirate here!"

Lucy shook her golden curls – just
as she always did when she was
showing off. She strutted off to find
the next clue.

Cat chewed some candyfloss. "Lucy won't share the booty," she said. "She'll keep it all to herself."

"Only if she finds it first," said Max. He spotted something through his telescope.

"Forget the clues," he said, pointing across the school field. "I think I know exactly where the treasure is hidden ..."

Sand Pit Treasure Dip

Pin the Tail on the Parrot

"The sandpit?" said Ant.

"Are you sure, Max?" Tiger asked.

"It does look a bit like a treasure island," said Cat. She looked through the telescope on her watch.

"And Miss Jones has sent everybody the other way to start with!" said Max.

All the other pirates were busy looking for clues. Max, Cat, Ant and Tiger walked briskly towards the sandpit.

"Look!" cried Cat. She pointed to a big X drawn in the sand. Max was right.

"What now?" asked Ant.

"We dig, of course," said Max.

"What if someone sees us?" said Cat.

"Yeah, someone like Lucy," growled Tiger.

Max looked at his friends and smiled. Cat sank her candyfloss stick into the sand. The four friends turned the dials on their watches and ...

The micro-friends began to dig.
It wasn't easy because they only
had their tiny wooden cutlasses. Tiger
wished he'd kept his ice-cream spoon.
Soon, their arms started to ache.
　　Suddenly, Ant's cutlass hit
something solid.

Over here!

"Over here!" he cried. "I think it's the treasure!"

All four of them fell to their knees. They could see something gold and shiny. They scooped at the sand with hoots of glee.

Just then, Tiger stopped digging. "Can anyone hear that?" he asked.

"What?" said Max, scooping up more sand.

There was a buzzing in the air.
The micro-friends stopped digging and
looked up. Dark shapes darted above
them. The buzzing got louder.

Tiger froze with terror.
Max's blood went cold. Cat squealed.
One tiny word came out of Ant's
mouth. It was … "Wasps!"
Max swiped at a wasp with his
cutlass. That just made the wasp cross.
Other wasps were zooming in fast.

"What are they after?" howled Tiger. "It's my candyfloss!" cried Cat. "The wasps are after my candyfloss! You lot stay here. I'll get rid of them."

Cat grabbed the
candyfloss stick.
She lifted it above
her head and sprinted
across the sand. The wasps
buzzed excitedly behind her.
On the far side of the sandpit,
she threw the stick with all her
strength. The candyfloss sailed through
the air like a javelin. The wasps
swarmed round it.

Chapter 4 - Treasure!

When Cat got back she gasped in surprise. Max, Ant and Tiger were grinning. Gold coins spilled out over the sand, each one glinting like a slice of sunshine.

"Chocolate coins," said Tiger. "Loads of them!"

"Don't forget the pirate code," said
Max. "We have to share the booty."

They took one coin each and rolled
them across the sand like wheels.

They clambered out over the side
of the sandpit just as a large shadow
loomed overhead.

Lucy looked down into the sandpit and her eyes lit up.

"The treasure!" she gloated. "And it's all mine!"

She picked up a handful of coins and tore one of them open. "My favourite," said Lucy, sniffing the sweet, chocolatey smell.

That's when she heard it – a loud buzzing sound ...

"Help!" cried Lucy, as the wasps swarmed round her. She clutched the coins in her hand and ran. The wasps followed her.

When the other pirates reached the sandpit there was treasure for everyone.

"How nice of Lucy to share all the booty," they said.